Adva

Cobwebs in ...
And How to Zap The Spider Who Made ...

All reviews below were submitted with express permission to be reprinted.

I have known Gayla Wood for more than ten years and in that time I have found her to be a committed follower of Christ who seeks to live out his will in her everyday life. She is contemplative, intuitive and creative, and those qualities are certainly seen in this book. *Cobwebs*... is an outgrowth of her journey into the likeness of Christ. As is seen in classes and at other gatherings, her heart is for the people of God to grow in their relationship with him. In this book she brings sound biblical principles to life through creative illustrations, mirroring her savior's penchant for parables. Using them she challenges us to look deep inside and be honest with ourselves and with our God. So much of our world is made up of fluff and façade, but she draws us from those surface things to examine our own processes of thinking regarding personal responsibility and guilt. Before we even have a chance to realize it, her humor has drawn us into an uncomfortable place that we might not have gone otherwise. Using many scriptures as her aid, we are brought face to face with the word of God and its transformative power in the life of a Christian. This is a book filled with advice that many Christians need to read and share with others. I am happily recommending it to others and to you.

TIMOTHY A. BUROW
DEAN OF INTERNATIONAL STUDIES
PRESIDENT-ELECT SUNSET INTERNATIONAL BIBLE INSTITUTE

Gayla Wood offers a straightforward guide for escaping the cobwebs of sin through prayer and submission to the will of God. She calls us to an honest confrontation of our acts, words, and motivations, and if needed, confession to God and those we have wronged. Healing, forgiveness, and restoration are possible through Christ, the Great Physician.

WOODY WOODROW, MDIV, MA, DMIN
AUSTIN GRADUATE SCHOOL OF THEOLOGY

In the Airport of Life, Gayla Wood is one of those committed to easing the travel of those waiting for the plane, and also to actively encouraging others to join in the journey. In this short book, she shares very practical advice, based upon Scripture, on key topics for the trip. From self-analysis, measured against Biblical teaching, to confession, forgiveness and moving on, she gives real life advice from her own study and experiences, and observations from her years as a teacher. This book is well worth the read, but be careful; you might find some of the words convicting!

PHIL PENDERGRAFT, ELDER
WOODLAND WEST CHURCH OF CHRIST
ARLINGTON, TX.

Reading *Cobwebs in the Christian Soul* is like settling in for a conversation with a sister who knows what you need to hear because she has swept the corners of her own soul. Gayla's "Action Steps" are presented in an encouraging manner with an air of expectation. She has confidence in her readers' ability to make things right because God has already done the heavy lifting. The questions at the end of each chapter are ideal for personal reflection or group discussion in a class study.

SANDI WOODROW
LICENSED PROFESSIONAL COUNSELOR

Cobwebs in the Christian Soul is a quick and easy read, yet it is a read that is deeply edifying and moves the Christian soul to do some spiritual house cleaning. Gayla Wood writes in a self-professed conversational style that weaves relatable illustrations which beautifully bring out the profound truths of the point she is making. *Cobwebs in the Christian Soul* is well worth reading devotionally or using as a small group study guide.

MIKE AND MAYRA BINGHAM
WOODLAND WEST CHURCH OF CHRIST IN ARLINGTON, TX.
MIKE SERVES AS YOUTH MINISTER.
MAYRA SERVES AS HIS RIGHT HAND.

Relatable analogies and spot-on guidance for Christians to take responsibility and move on from their own and other's mistakes and sins. Concrete Scripture-based examples and thought-provoking questions walk one on a journey of becoming closer to God. Great book for an individual or Bible Study group, whether New Christians or seasoned church members.

LINDA CARRIER

ENVIRONMENTAL SPECIALIST

OWNER, GENGREEN E-COMMERCE

Gayla Wood will hold your attention as she guides you on a journey of self-examination and (re)discovery of the roles that Forgiveness, Prayer, and the Church play in our daily walk with God. Written in an easy-to-read conversational style prose with a little lighthearted whimsical humor, you'll be caught off guard to suddenly find yourself in a state of deep intellectual introspection. Based on solid biblical principles, Gayla includes many supporting scriptural references interspersed throughout the text. The end of each chapter includes thought-provoking questions that are suitable for both personal consideration as well as facilitating an interactive group study. I strongly recommend this book regardless of where you are in your journey with Christ; the depth of wisdom found herein will comfort, encourage, and inspire you at every stage along the way.

BERT JOHNSON

PROGRAM PLANNING AND SCHEDULING MANAGER

Cobwebs is a beautifully written, engaging self-help book that will be enjoyed by new Christians as well as those who grew up in the faith. Wood's conversational style makes for a quick read, and it will leave the reader with introspection, forced to take a closer look at his/her own motivations, thoughts, and actions, especially in the face of temptations to minimize sin in one's own life. Her biblically sound and well-documented book addresses very serious topics with just the right amount of humor, and will leave you anxiously anticipating her next book and rereading this one in the meantime.

LARKA L. TETENS, M.ED.; L.P.C.
TETENS COUNSELING CENTER
ARLINGTON, TEXAS

Fantastic piece of work by a highly talented and strong Christian woman! Gayla Wood's *Cobwebs in the Christian Soul* is a must read, and an excellent addition to your personal bible study library. I would highly recommend this book for your personal and spiritual development.

ROBERT H. TAYLOR
COMMAND SERGEANT MAJOR USA/RET
NORTHERN LIGHTS CHURCH OF CHRIST
FAIRBANKS, ALASKA

Cobwebs in the Christian Soul

COBWEBS IN THE CHRISTIAN SOUL

And How to Zap The Spider Who Made Them

Gayla Wood

ELM HILL

A Division of
HarperCollins Christian Publishing

www.elmhillbooks.com

Cobwebs in the Christian Soul
And How to Zap The Spider Who Made Them

Published in Nashville, Tennessee, by Elm Hill, an imprint of Thomas Nelson. Elm Hill and Thomas Nelson are registered trademarks of HarperCollins Christian Publishing, Inc.

Elm Hill titles may be purchased in bulk for educational, business, fund-raising, or sales promotional use. For information, please e-mail SpecialMarkets@ ThomasNelson.com.

Library of Congress Cataloging-in-Publication Data

Library of Congress Control Number: 2018953073

ISBN 978-1-595559098 (Paperback)
ISBN 978-1-595559173 (Hardbound)
ISBN 978-1-595559081 (eBook)

DEDICATION AND THANKS

This book is dedicated to my mom, Gail Ellis,
who taught me to pray. She was also the very first person
to ever ask me to write a story.

Additionally, I want to thank some people
who are very important to me:

My husband, Mark Wood, for believing in my dream to
become a writer, even when I sometimes doubted myself

My dad, Cotton Ellis, for being a sounding board and
a constant compass, in seas both rough and calm

My daughter, Sarah, who whispers wisdom beyond her years

Sarah's husband Bryan and their children Micah, Eisley,
Shepherd, and Paige, for being perpetual blessings
to me and to this family

Tim Burow, Woody and Sandi Woodrow, Phil Pendergraft, Mike
and Mayra Bingham, Bert Johnson, Larka Tetens,
and Rob Taylor for writing reviews for this book

Mary Jo Cochrum, for offering sage insights about feelings,
forgiveness, and forgetting

And to my two Linda's...
-Linda Carrier, thank you for writing a review for this book
and for decades of patiently listening to almost
everything I have ever written.

-Linda Malone, you were the first person other than
my parents to ask me to read a whole book out loud to you.
Thank you for encouraging me, believing in me,
and for seeing past recent roadblocks when I did not.

But MOST IMPORTANTLY, I want to thank my God
who has supplied my every need,
every single day of my life!

~Gayla

This book is intended to be a <u>general approach</u> to daily Christian Living, but some situations are extremely specific, extremely time-sensitive, and extremely personal. A few items on that list are: Marital Infidelity, Abuse, Addiction, Victimization, and Indecency with/Harm to a Child.

Areas of an extreme and personal nature require the assistance and guidance of professionals. **<u>Please seek immediate assistance if you or others you know are either currently being harmed/victimized or are in danger of being harmed/victimized.</u>**

Greetings to My Christian Siblings,

This book is presented in a straightforward and conversational style. Each chapter is scripturally based. Each concept is simple to understand. The problem-solving action steps regarding the Christian issues discussed here are user-friendly. But I caution you that breaking old habits takes dedication and stamina. These action steps are not for the fainthearted, for they ask us to delve past the surface of our daily interactions and get to the heart of how honest we really are with ourselves, with others, and with our God.

From personal experience, I can state that <u>understanding</u> God's will in my life is often far easier than <u>submitting</u> to His will in my life. Like so many life lessons, I've learned the action steps that you will read about in this book the hard way. They did NOT first appear as I see them today. They appeared as anxiety, sleeplessness, bad dreams, dysfunctional relationships, buckets of tears and diminished health.

Amazingly, when I got right with God, the action steps came into focus.

Like I said, I learned these steps the hard way.

"Therefore, since we are surrounded by such a great cloud of witnesses, let us throw off everything that hinders and the sin that so <u>easily entangles</u>. And let us run with perseverance the race marked out for us."

Hebrews 12:1 (NIV®)

Sin, like Cobwebs, can easily entangle us. And just like when we walk through an actual cobweb and are then simply overcome with the urgency to get that sticky stuff off our bodies, the spiritual equivalent should occur. When we find that *The Spider* has managed to weave a spiritual cobweb in our soul, we should be overcome with the same urgency to be rid of it immediately. *The Spider* watches in eager anticipation of the chance to drag souls back into his darkness.

I pray that as you read this book, you will find insight and tools to use in your spiritual journey. I pray that it will, in some measure, help equip you to help others in their journeys too. May God bless you richly as you seek His Will.

At the onset, I think it wise to share with you the Christian common-ground statements that are "the givens" in this book. They are as follows:

- **There ARE some Absolute Truths in this world: the <u>first</u> is that God exists!**

   (*You can argue this all day long if you are so inclined, but you'll only be flappin' your gums. God Exists!*)

- **<u>A second Absolute Truth</u> is that Jesus Christ died as the perfect sacrifice for the sins of the world, was raised from the dead three days later, and ascended into heaven where he sits at the right hand of God Almighty.**

- **<u>A third Absolute Truth</u> is that the Holy Spirit is sent to dwell within Christians. He comforts us, guides us, and interprets our innermost feelings to God Himself.**

- **<u>A fourth Absolute Truth</u> is that once all of our sins are forgiven, it is only a matter of time until we will sin again.** And herein lies the crux of this book—sin happens! *The*

Spider wants to trap us, and he spins various and sundry webs to try to do so. Satan's cobwebs are waiting for us all.

Five Initial *Spider*-Zapping Steps:

1. Immediately go to God in prayer to ask forgiveness. **(1 John 1:9)**
2. Ask forgiveness from those whom we may have negatively impacted. **(Matthew 5:23–24)**
3. Pray for the strength to avoid sinful thoughts, words, and deeds. **(1 Corinthians 10:14)**
4. Focus on the scriptures that tell us how to think, speak, and act. **(Galatians 5:22-23)**
5. Pray for the ability to discern and purposefully follow God's Will. **(Colossians 1:9–10)**

These five steps are spiritually healthy. They are scripturally based. This is how it is supposed to work.

But sometimes *The Spider's* webs entangle us.

The blood of Christ does continually clean us **(1 John 1:7)**, but sometimes we lose our focus.

Sometimes we neglect our prayers.

Sometimes we just get all wrapped up in *The Spider's* web.

When that happens, we may tend to obsess about how we were wronged or how we woefully wronged someone else. It is significant to note that in such times it is apparent that our minds have been focusing on our yesterdays and our tomorrows, instead of simply looking up to Christ who is our RIGHT NOW.

Precious life energy is wasted by engaging in unworthy mindsets.

Instead of exercising our faith, we can get engaged in fighting the tangles of Satan's webs. Instead of feeling free in Christ, we can feel trapped by *The Spider*.

God-loving Christian people can sometimes just get totally stuck in those webs.

The Spider's webs are sticky like that.

A Christian who is spiderweb-stuck may end up resigned to <u>feeling</u> sin-stained, sullied, and quite adrift from Jesus. Sadly, some folks end up <u>feeling</u> that getting back to righteousness is completely beyond them.

FEELINGS are always legitimate, but the perceptions and information behind our feelings can sometimes be based on one of *The Spiders'* LIES! *The Spider* lies quite often. It's his favorite "GO-TO" move, as well as his most reliable cobweb-slinging trick. He can flick a lie at us faster than lightning! Therefore, if we are not watchful, his lies can clog up our thinking, which can then in turn impact our feelings.

The Bible clearly tells us how to get back to righteousness. The Bible tells us exactly what to do. What I am sharing with you is not new; these ideas are already in The Bible.

Yet in many churches today there are people who feel spiritually miserable because they have been attacked by Satan's Spiritual Spiderwebs.

Here's how it happens: Some wrong word or deed occurs and the next thing you know *The Spider* is attempting to set up housekeeping in your soul. And he always brings his darkness with him; things like hopelessness, anger, misery, isolation, rejection, worthlessness, jealousy, revenge, and apathy.

But we are not of the dark. We are Children of Light.

"For you were once darkness, but now you are light in the Lord. Live as children of light."

Ephesians 5:8 (NIV*)

Clearly, Satan wants to alienate us from God, and he is using our own minds to do so.

Because of that, this book is needed.

Because of that, this book was written.

The action steps below indicate what we, as Christians, are supposed to do when we come face to face with our own human errors and find **Cobwebs in the Christian Soul**.

1. Mess Up?
2. 'Fess Up!
3. Fix It! (Even If You Can't, God Can!)
4. Move On
5. Live Better=Pray and Study God's Word
6. Be Actively Engaged in the Church

So there you have it: six simple chapters based on six simple concepts. Let's get started!

In Him,
Gayla Wood

CONTENTS

Your Status Check

MESS UP?

*This chapter is about the Awareness of Messing Up,
also known as experiencing "it".*

Sometimes you are waiting for **it,** actively looking for **it,** because you know **it** is lurking. You know **it** is coming. And even with all your skills sharpened, somehow **it** still manages to hit you square on the head like an Acme cartoon anvil.

But there are other times when you think all is well. Life is grand. Things are great. And just about that time, **it** slips under the back door as an unseen vapor and starts to materialize. **It** takes a while to materialize before your eyes, but when **it** is fully formed you realize what **it** is; and fear settles in your belly in a hard knot. In this scenario as well, **it** manages to hit you square on the head like an Acme cartoon anvil.

The Awareness of Messing Up and having **it** come after us can be quite scary. Because, as we all know, **it** can take many forms:

It may be an Accident that Occurred.

It may be a Malicious Intent Revealed.

It may be a Partially True but Mostly False Accusation Endured.

But most commonly, **It** turns out to be that Sudden Guilty Feeling.

Do you remember an event in which one or maybe even both of your parents suddenly bellowed out your whole name? Mine sounded something like this: "Gayla Ray Ellis *(Ellis was my maiden name)*, you better get your little hiney-bottom in here quick!"

As an aside, I have never understood why my parents always summoned just my hiney-bottom rather than all of me. Obviously, in order for my hiney-bottom to arrive, the rest of me had to get there too! Right? Or perhaps it was because the hiney-bottom part was really the only part of me that had to be present for the spanking to occur. After all, they knew I was a smart child, so maybe they figured I might go hide my hiney-bottom real good... and with no hiney, there could be no spanking.... and if there was no spanking, they must've feared I'd get away with my heinous childhood crimes against humanity!

Anyway, by the time I could get to wherever "here" was, I was already panicked and wondering what I had done. But this much was always true: by the time me and my *hiney-bottom* arrived, the **It** had already dropped the Acme cartoon anvil on my head.

As a child, I assumed that if one of my parents called me in this fashion, I MUST HAVE done something wrong. If their tone and word usage indicated that I was guilty, I WAS.

If the accusation was made, I was inherently guilty because my parents SAID I was.

For some people, that inherently guilty childhood response pattern stays intact for the rest of their lives.

"If someone **said** I did it, I must be guilty."

The title of this chapter is **"Did I Mess Up?"** and yes, that question is intentional. One of the best spiritual tools you can ever develop is the ability to freeze the moment, disregard whatever potential penalties exist, and honestly answer the question of **"Did I Mess Up?"**

Take a look at these four questions:

1. Are you able to <u>biblically</u> assess your own guilt or innocence in a given situation?
2. Do you thoroughly examine your <u>actions</u>, <u>words</u>, and <u>private motivations</u> in a biblically-based self-assessment process?
3. When the question of whether or not you have Messed Up presents itself, do you <u>always</u> go through a biblically-based self-assessment and examine your own <u>actions</u>, <u>words</u>, and <u>private motivations</u>?
4. Do you just instinctively ALWAYS do what is right?

Let's see how you scored!

<u>GRADING KEY</u>:

-   If you answered YES to all four questions → Congratulations! Welcome to Sainthood! Put this book down! *(And go get a mirror, because I suspect that you will soon be sprouting a Pinocchio nose.)*

- However, if you answered NO to two or more of these questions → Congratulations! You show honesty and are probably like the rest of us; flawed, but trying. Most of us probably answered "Sometimes" to questions 1 and 2. Like I said, we tend to be flawed but trying.
- However, some folks refuse to self-assess at all costs. This can be for a whole host of reasons ranging anywhere from bull-headed-corn-bread-arrogance to deep-seated-anxiety-laced-issues needing professional help.

Bottom Line: Don't Judge!

We never really know what is going on in the hearts and heads of others.

God Knows.

But We Do Not!!!

At this point I should probably also mention that some folks are all too eager to self-assess, because they hunger for the chance to prove to others that they are *Innocents in a Bad, Bad World* and thus want to completely exonerate themselves of their own guilt in their own eyes and all others' eyes. I have found that these types are often quite gifted at finding inventive word-ways to wiggle out of and avoid personal accountability.

But pish-posh, I digress....

Whatever your score in this little honesty assessment, you have now taken the first step.

You have remembered that guilt and innocence are biblically determinable. You have remembered that God sees our actions, words, and private motivations. And you have remembered that biblical innocence is the goal.

If you have been accused of "Messing Up," have examined your-self biblically (*actions, words, and private motivations*), and have found that you come up clean, Praise God.

You are off the hook!

Your task now is to avoid acting cocky and spoiling it.

"A gentle answer turns away wrath, but a harsh word stirs up anger."

Proverbs 15:1 (NIV•)

- Guard your mouth at this point.
- Guard your actions.
- Guard your private motivations.
- Strive to be a polite, kind, and gracious person regardless of the false accusation.
- Just because you were wrongly accused does NOT give you a license to spew sarcasm.
- Trash talk does NOT bring glory to God.

But what happens when you've been accused of "Messing Up," and after biblically examining your actions, words, and private motiva-tions, you can see that in the grand scheme of things, it is REMOTELY possible that you might be considered by some people to be just a wee tad, *or perhaps better yet, just a skosh,* guilty?

Come on now! Guilt is Guilt!! OWN IT!!!

The Bible points to a two-part answer to this. You need to "'Fess Up":

1. Confess your sin to God and ask for His forgiveness.
2. Confess your sin to the person you offended and ask for her/ his forgiveness.

Chapter 1 Questions for Personal Reflection and Analysis:

A. Did I do something wrong knowingly? Unknowingly? Accidentally?

B. Who knows about it?

C. If I did, how do I feel? (Angry? Guilty? Ashamed? Proud?)

D. Are my feelings biblically appropriate?

E. Do others think I am guilty when actually I am innocent?

F. Please evaluate why and consider options for future encounters.

G. Do others think I am innocent when I am really guilty?

H. Please evaluate why and consider options for future encounters.

I. How do I define *guilt* and *innocence*?

J. Do I believe in degrees of guilt? Why?

K. Do I believe in degrees of innocence? Why?

L. Do I have the correct spirit in this matter?

M. Do I think God would agree with my assessment of the situation? Why?

N. What scriptures did you use as you answered these questions?

Chapter 1 NOTES:

Action Step

'FESS UP

How do we learn about confession?
How do we learn to ask forgiveness?
Big concepts for consideration in this chapter:
Confession, Debt, Forgiveness, Punishment, Fear, Trust,
Grace, Mercy, Discipline, and Character.

I have always heard that "Confession is Good for the Soul!" Is it really? In this context, I think that Confession really translates as Honesty. And so YES, Honesty IS good for the soul.

Parents spend countless hours trying to teach honesty to their children. They often say things like "Breaking the lamp is bad, but breaking the lamp and then lying about it is twice as bad; and will get twice the punishment. Who broke the lamp? Did you break the lamp?"

Consider kid A: She's a cool customer. Been down this road before. She is thinking… *Ok, before I answer anything, I need to know two things:*

1. *What does "twice the punishment" really mean?*
2. *And what exactly IS the punishment that I am gonna get twice as much of if I confess right now?*

We have all seen families like this and know that at this point it's a horse race:

"And They're OFF...Honesty just threw her rider and stopped to chew grass.
Trust never got out of the gate.
Self-preservation and **Trying to Get Out of This** are neck and neck.
It's gonna be close! They are approaching the finish line.
...and **Trying to Get Out of This** wins by a nose."

In this type of situation, where it is very clear that a misdeed has occurred (*clearly, the lamp is broken*), generally the Fear of Punishment aspect has been emphasized far more than the Joy of Forgiveness aspect. Either one of them, taken by themselves, is not what God intended; they work in tandem. He knew we needed to experience both the Fear of Punishment and the Joy of Forgiveness in order to fully appreciate both aspects.

Too often we fail to accurately demonstrate the delicate and dynamic relationship between these two opposite concepts. We sometimes offer Forgiveness easily so that our children will not endure guilt. Or just the opposite, we sometimes emphasize the Fear of Punishment in hopes that maybe Fear will cause our children to avoid making bad choices.

Parents have such a difficult and important job. We provide our babies the background lessons from which they will come to know God and His Plan of Salvation. Therefore it is clear that they need to learn both the Fear of Punishment AND the Joy of Forgiveness.

When children are small and their transgressions are small, we seem to emphasize grace, mercy, and forgiveness. We model the spirit of gentleness. But children do not stay small, nor do their transgressions. Appropriate Boundaries must be clearly defined and Appropriate Consequences must be established. In this way, our children learn personal integrity, accountability, self-discipline, and character.

As adults we need to be mindful that biblical forgiveness does not mean that the slate is **simply** wiped clean. Sins are forgiven, but at great cost—the blood of Christ. **(Galatians 3:13–15)**

Biblical forgiveness is not a casual oopsy-daisy process. Jesus died because of our sins.

Children need to know what it means when we say that we forgive them. When an adult offers *forgiveness* to a child who can comprehend the meaning of the word, it is important to convey what the word *DOES MEAN* as well as what it **DOES NOT MEAN.**

These days, offering *forgiveness* to someone tends to mean that our adrenal system is calm, our emotions are stable, we love them, and we bear them no ill will. All of which is hopefully true. But if that is all that we teach our children we have short-circuited the lesson.

It is also essential to teach our children that the being *forgiven* does not take away the logical consequences of wrongful actions.

Here's a quick script that illustrates this truth:

> "I *forgive* you for breaking the lamp and am no longer angry with you. However, there is still the matter of the consequence of your actions. This was not just a simple accident. You were playing

football in the house when you know you are not allowed to do
so. Therefore, you are responsible for replacing the broken lamp
with a comparable lamp."

This is how we teach responsibility.
This is how we teach respect for other's property.
This is how we teach children to do the right thing.

Logical consequences are powerful tools.
Logical consequences are also Biblical tools.

David was a man after God's Own Heart **(1 Samuel 13:14)**, but
he still had to live with the consequences of his sin with Bathsheba **(2
Samuel 12:10-14)**. Nathan the prophet told David that as a consequence of his sin, adversity would be raised up from within his own
house. And that adversary turned out to be his own son Absalom. Each
act of defiance by Absalom must have been a constant reminder to
David of the time he strayed from God's will.

Our children must be taught that forgiveness does not mean a lack
of accountability. They need to know that when they do something
wrong, there is a debt that must be paid.

In the broken lamp scenario, perhaps a child might need to do
extra chores to *work off* the price of replacing the lamp. These are
golden opportunities to teach life lessons to children. Through a child's
"Mess Ups," we can teach Forgiveness, Mercy, and Grace when we first
teach them to "'Fess Up."

But all of those are meaningless unless children are taught to
understand the significance of Forgiveness, Mercy, and Grace. You
cannot fully understand light unless you have experienced darkness.

And a child cannot understand forgiveness unless he has experienced guilt.

By the way, I have been conveniently discussing this topic as it relates to children, but in reality I have been leading up to mentioning that it's the same with those of us who are grown. WE must understand guilt before we can understand forgiveness too.

Forgiveness is a gift. But Forgiveness has a price. Sometimes we decide to not make someone pay that price (*this is mercy*), but it doesn't negate the fact that there was a price. A broken lamp is easily replaced. The stakes change drastically when kids gets older. It is highly likely that most parents will contend with an apparent lack of logic used in adolescent decision-making, issues of broken trust, and some personal safety issues. The potential negative impacts of poor decisions increase with the age of the kid.

Wise Christian parents tend to:

- Start teaching these lessons early and often.
- Teach with wisdom, love, and biblical consistency.

If we fail to establish the concept of biblical guilt and innocence in our children, they grow up thinking that they can avoid accountability; which can be a spiritually crippling issue. It is essential that a biblical sense of accountability is gently and lovingly cultivated in each of us. We must all experience the discomfort of acknowledging our sins, **before** we can understand that Jesus gave his life to pay the debt for our sins.

People need to comprehend their Guilt and Pending Eternal Punishment in Hell to be able to fully comprehend their Forgiveness and Pending Eternal Reward in Heaven.

Biblical Forgiveness means that the debt has been paid and the account ledger is balanced. This is what Jesus did when he died for our sins. OUR sins were OUR debts. And OUR sin-debts separate us from God and resign us to *The Spider* called Satan.

Since we have all sinned **(Romans 3:23)**, at one time we were ALL in Satan's clutches. If Jesus Christ had not agreed to take our place, and thus die in our place as the perfect sacrifice for our sins, we would have all been doomed to hell.

Christ's lifeblood was the price necessary to balance the ledger and get you and me out of Beelzebub's Pawnshop window!

Our children too often fail to hear their parents explain forgiveness in this manner.

Fortunately, most adults have gotten some form of that lesson somewhere along the line. As adults we grasp the difference between breaking a lamp (*Accident*) and the exposed lie that was used to try to cover it up (*Malicious Intent Revealed*).

We KNOW those are two different things. But interestingly enough, adults sometimes act just like children; we sometimes try to get away from guilt by choosing to tell a lie. Meanwhile, members of our society have become incredible Tolerators; most likely to avoid the probability of being seen as Intolerant. We rarely tell another grown person that we know that they have told a lie. And if we do let them know that we perceive their lack of honesty, we certainly don't say the word Liar to them, because that would be construed as labeling and name calling, both of which are really big societal No-Nos.

Alas, tolerating has too often been construed as endorsing. Metaphorically speaking, we may have to tolerate the smell of a dirty diaper in a nearby trash can. But it seems as if some people fear being labeled as intolerant (*and thus **socially unacceptable***) to the degree that they feel obligated not only to sniff the dirty diaper but also to applaud it.

And when was the last time, other than in an actual courtroom, that you heard anybody *(well, anybody who is not associated with politics and mudslinging)* say that someone is guilty of something? It might have been a very long time. Guilt *(with the obvious exception of notorious celebrities)* is not openly discussed very much anymore.

But guilt, to varying degrees, is an ongoing state for most us. Most of us have never been taken to court, yet we are guilty of breaking all sorts of rules and/or laws.

For example, let's talk about Speeding.

Person X may be guilty of habitually exceeding the posted speed limit when driving, but generally folks don't say she is guilty of being a habitual lawbreaker. Instead, we tend to rationalize that situation so that if it is discussed among others at all, the negative connotation is usually removed, making it sound something like, *"She has a heavy foot!"*

We put a cute spin on it, because today it is pretty much considered ***politically incorrect*** to speak words or write words indicating that someone is **guilty** of anything.

These days, most adult individuals of our society will avoid being seen as ***intolerant and thus socially unacceptable*** and/or ***politically incorrect*** at almost all costs. But why? Why are we hesitant to acknowledge and identify bad behavior? Why do we protect it? Why do we neutralize it and call it a character flaw or an unfortunate personality trait? Why indeed!

Well, there IS the whole probability of Slander and Malice legalities with which to wrestle. And yes, we in the United States ARE an extremely litigious society.

But I submit that there is likely another rationale at play, and it goes like this:

*"When **you** are guilty and **I** know it (but I don't tell on you), and when **I** am guilty and **you** know it (but you don't tell on me either), we create a mutually beneficial alliance in which we both get to continue doing whatever bad things we want to do, without penalty, for a very long time."*

But we know this alliance has a finite shelf life.

"For there is nothing hidden that will not be disclosed, and nothing concealed that will not be known or brought out into the open."

LUKE 8:17 (NIV*)

Perhaps this little story will help focus my point.

I once knew a woman who always kept her toenails polished, but also developed a fungal infection in one toenail. One day when changing her polish color, she noticed that there was a black dot on the toenail of the big toe on her right foot. She dismissed the dot by repainting her toenails with the new color and went along her way.

The following month she treated herself to a pedicure and was nearly embarrassed to death when the nail technician yelped in alarm at the dark fungal infection on that toenail. And even worse, the ladies in the chairs next to her saw the technician's reaction and then saw her ugly toenail for themselves. They gasped. She fled with unpolished toes.

Though she had left the nail salon in shame, her shame was insufficient to motivate her to make the wise decision to call her doctor about the infection. Instead she went home, polished her own toenails, and covered up the problem once again.

Infection out of sight. Infection out of mind.

Several months later she realized that her toenail was coming loose. When she removed the polish on that toe, she saw that the black area was more than halfway up the nail.

You'd think she would have gone to the doctor by this time, but no; instead, she scoured the internet to find an easy fix. She decided to soak it in saltwater; but only did so a few times and not for very long. She tried to justify herself by mumbling out loud that she was a busy woman who didn't have time to sit about soaking her foot in saltwater.

Funny how you and I can see that she was only seeking social acceptability when she really needed true healing; but true healing was nowhere on her agenda ... yet.

Predictably, the fungus continued to grow.

Still she did not exercise wisdom.

Still she did not go visit her physician.

Instead, she consulted her hairstylist who told her to mix one part bleach to three parts water, and to flush this solution under the loose nail. She followed her stylist's sage advice.

But the fungal infection was deeply entrenched by now and her folksy halfhearted attempts were useless. She was doing too little too late.

Finally she went to her physician. He prescribed a one month supply of antifungal pills. She was elated. This was the quick fix that she had been looking for. But true to her "busy woman" form, she skipped more than a few doses of her medication, while more layers of toenail polish were liberally applied. Exactly one month after her doctor visit, she took off her toenail polish and finally took a long honest look at the infected toenail.

She was utterly disgusted by what she saw and grabbed the nearest pair of nail scissors. Carefully, she cut away the decaying part of the toenail and then she called her physician. He prescribed another month-long round of the antifungal medication.

But this time, she was diligent. She took the pills every day. She also flushed the area four times a day with the bleach and water solution. She no longer applied polish to her toenails; no more trying to cover it up. And she carefully tended to the problem.

It took a very long time, but eventually the toenail grew back healthy and complete.

Isn't the story of this woman and her physical infection similar to what happens with people who have an area of spiritual infection?

At first they try to ignore it and cover it up. They get upset when other people discover that something isn't right. They give halfhearted attempts at changing their habits. And then finally, when they are disgusted at themselves, they seek the Great Physician.

This is exactly the way sin tends to work in our lives. We tend to want to hide it. We tend to want to cover it up. When others find out about it and are shocked we get upset, but often not sufficiently to cause us to seek true and lasting change. Too often it takes us a long time to really understand that we cannot heal ourselves and that we need the Great Physician.

Christ IS the Great Physician. He cleans us. He heals us. He takes away our sins. But we must always remember that it is the perpetual nature of mankind to sin. And sin, left unchecked, creates spiritual infection. Deliberate action is required.

"What shall we say, then? Shall we go on sinning so that grace may increase? By no means! We are those who have died to sin; how can we live in it any longer?"

ROMANS 6:1–2 (NIV°)

How similar to that woman are we?

We have open access to the Great Physician but too often we determine that it is not necessary to Consult Him or Seek the Cure.

Christ can forgive us, but just like when the woman in the story cut away the decaying part of her nail, we too must take action to make real changes. Christians must separate ourselves from infectious things. We must be willing to cut away, dispose of, and reject the things that cause spiritual disease.

We must be willing to obey what scripture says.

"Woe to the world because of the things that cause people to stumble! Such things must come, but woe to the person through whom they come! If your hand or your foot causes you to stumble, cut it off and throw it away. It is better for you to enter life maimed or crippled than to have two hands or two feet and be thrown into eternal fire. And if your eye causes you to stumble, gouge it out and throw it away. It is better for you to enter life with one eye than to have two eyes and be thrown into the fire of hell."

MATTHEW 18:7–9 (NIV°)

This scripture is not leading us to physically harm ourselves. It is leading us to spiritually purge from our lives the things that cause us to sin. It asks us to change our life patterns. It calls us to choose God's way over our way. Changing life patterns can take time. Ask any reformed gambler, drug addict, smoker, drinker, liar, gossiper.... I could go on and on. The reality here is that the list of these things would eventually engulf us all. The sinful things we think, say, and do lead us to the sinful results we find so appalling.

That is why it is so important to keep the things we think, say, and do centered on the things we find in God's Word.

"Finally, brothers and sisters, whatever is true, whatever is noble, whatever is right, whatever is pure, whatever is lovely, whatever is admirable—if anything is excellent or praiseworthy—think about such things. Whatever you have learned or received or heard from me, or seen in me—put it into practice. And the God of peace will be with you."

PHILIPPIANS 4:8–11 (NIV®)

Chapter 2 Questions for Personal Reflection and Analysis:

A. Does honesty have a price?

B. Has the price ever been too high or too low for you personally?

C. How did you learn to confess?

D. How did you learn to ask forgiveness?

E. Can asking forgiveness ever be offensive to the one being asked? Why? How?

F. What is the Biblical response to someone who refuses to forgive you?

G. How often do you confess your actions, words, and private motivations to God?

H. Can you recall a time when you asked forgiveness of God?

I. Has there ever been a time when you felt as if forgiveness was denied?

J. Why do you think might have happened?

K. What did you do?

L. Did you take any additional action?

M. Did you go back a second time and ask forgiveness from God?

N. If so, what was the result?

O. What did you learn?

P. Can you recall a time when you asked forgiveness of someone important to you?

Q. Are we accountable to be honest to family members? Church members? Strangers we encounter?

R. What scriptures did you use as you answered these questions?

Chapter 2 NOTES:

CHAPTER 3

Action Step

FIX IT!
(EVEN IF YOU CAN'T,
GOD CAN!)

Have you realized yet that we are working through a system here? Has it hit you yet that simply admitting that you have done wrong is not sufficient? Have you come to the understanding that simply confessing that you made a mistake is not the end of the story? Why is it that people sometimes think that once they surrender their pride enough to admit wrongdoing, everyone is obligated to let bygones be bygones? No one is immune from mistakes. And really, how fragile must a person's self-esteem be if even in small matters he or she can never admit errors? But I digress yet again...

L et's bring this point home.
Let's say that I came to your home and you showed me your collection of stamps, or baseball cards, or china teacups or whatever it might be, and I damaged one of them.

Wouldn't you expect me to offer to replace it?

Wouldn't you expect me to offer to buy you another one or minimally offer to pay you the value of what I broke?

Of course you would.

You might be a kind person and not accept the offer from me, but wouldn't you feel much better if I offered?

See, that's the way it's supposed to be. If you damage a thing, you need to try to correct that damage. It's far easier to do this with things than it is with people. When we damage things, there are processes for repair and/or replacement.

But when we damage another human, be it emotionally, mentally, physically, or all of the above, restitution is not so easily dispatched.

Admitting that you made a mistake is a huge part. Confessing your regrets about that and acknowledging that you handled something all together inappropriately is still only part of making things right.

Try telling the other person what you have learned about this situation and how you would approach things differently if you had the chance. Be specific. Let them see that you learned something from this encounter.

Then ask their forgiveness.

They may or may not forgive you. They do have a choice. It would be better for them personally if they do forgive you. (**Matthew 18: 21–35, Mark 11:25, Ephesians 4:26**) Yet, they may not; you need to be prepared for whichever way they choose to handle the situation.

In a perfect world, they would forgive you and everything would be wonderful. But we don't live in a perfect world. They are not perfect and neither are you; otherwise you would never have messed up in the first place, right?

So if they forgive you, Praise Jesus.

HINT: Don't confuse forgiving with forgetting! These two concepts are not the same; in fact, they are very different.

(*We will talk more about the difference between these two concepts in Chapter 4.*)

But if they do not forgive you, respect their decision and still Praise Jesus. Do not add insult to injury and exacerbate the situation with a lot of loud talk or "huffin and puffin" (*as my grandmother used to call it*).

Simply let go of it.

Pray for them.

Ask God to soften their heart so that they will know that you are truly sorry.

You may need to give them time. You may need to leave them alone for a while. You may need to let God work on them in His way. **(Hebrews 4:12)**

Then perhaps you may be able to approach that person again one day down the road, after God has softened the person's heart.

But if you have truly asked God to forgive you and you have given a good and faithful effort to make certain that you apologized to the person that you offended (*even possibly repeatedly*), then let it go.

Hand this situation over to God.

"Set your mind on things above, not on earthly things."

Colossians 3:2 (NIV·)

Do not linger in the garden of discontent. Do not bask in being an unforgiven person. God loves you; take comfort in the fact that you tried to do the right thing.

Simply let it go.

Release the pain and the guilt.

Learn from your mistake.

Remember the way that your wrong choice negatively impacted the other person and yourself, but do not walk around wearing former guilt like a stinky gym sweatshirt.

Toss it and Move On.

Before closing this chapter, I do want to mention **once again** that there are some situations that do not readily conform to the Mess Up?, 'Fess Up, Fix It, and Move On methodology.

This book is intended to be a general approach to daily Christian Living, but some situations are extremely specific, extremely time-sensitive, and extremely personal. A few items on that list are: Marital Infidelity, Abuse, Addiction, Victimization, and Indecency with/Harm to a Child.

Areas of an extreme and personal nature require the assistance and guidance of professionals. **Please seek immediate assistance if you or others you know are either currently being harmed/victimized or are in danger of being harmed/victimized.**

Chapter 3 Questions for Personal Reflection and Analysis:

A. Did your parents <u>model</u> the "'Fess Up & Fix It" approach when <u>they</u> made mistakes?

B. Can you remember a specific time they either did so, or that you wish they would have done so?

C. How did their example(s) impact the way that you respond to discovering that you have done something wrong?

D. Can you think of a time when you did not admit that you were wrong?

E. Can you describe what happened?

F. What were the consequences?

G. If you had the chance, would you change anything about that scenario?

H. Can you think of a time when someone forgave you?

I. How did you feel prior to that forgiveness?

J. How did you feel after?

K. Have you ever forgiven someone you love of doing something that hurt you deeply?

L. If so, how did that feel for you?

M. How did it feel for them?

N. Have you ever refused to forgive someone?

O. Is there an emotional price for refusing to forgive? If so, please describe.

P. Is there ever a physical price for refusing to forgive? If so, please describe.

Q. Is there a spiritual price for refusing to forgive? If so, please describe.

R. What does the Bible say about Forgiveness? Please base these responses on actual scriptures. Feel free to look them up right now.

S. Has there ever been a time when you were forgiven but still had a consequence?

T. Has there ever been a time when you forgave someone else but there was still a consequence that the person had to endure?

U. What scriptures did you use as you answered these questions?

Chapter 3 NOTES:

CHAPTER 4

Action Step

MOVE ON

Simply put: Cobwebs in the Christian Soul are very sticky and gum up our minds. And those Cobwebs have Cousins, one of whom is called Spiritual Quicksand. We step into Spiritual Quicksand when we fail to acknowledge that by the Blood of Christ our sins have been forgiven. Some people do not forgive at all, and some people are just really slow about doing so. God did not call you to live in a spirit of fear **(Romans 8:15)** *He has called us to do our best to resolve conflicts and then move on!* **(Romans 12:18)**

Stepping back in that unforgiven mindset is like shunning God's Grace and Jesus' Sacrifice to save us. It's a big deal when people get stuck in Spiritual Quicksand.

Consider the following fellow:

- He was baptized for the forgiveness of his sins and received the gift of the Holy Spirit.
- He was leading a faithful life.
- Then one day he stepped off the spiritual path and sinned in a big and public way.
- He realized the error of his ways and confessed that sin to God.
- He asked God's forgiveness and asked forgiveness from the person he sinned against.
- He was restored and got back on the right spiritual path
- And then shortly thereafter he stepped right into Spiritual Quicksand <u>because ultimately he could not forgive himself of his sins. He just couldn't get past it.</u>
- The man got bogged down and simply could not move on.

When I was a kid, my friends and I used to love to watch the TV show *Tarzan*. It seemed like there was always some poor soul who stepped into the quicksand pit.

Even as kids we knew that if you flop around in quicksand, you are going to sink. TV taught us that to get out of quicksand you have to make slow and smooth movements. We saw that you had to concentrate hard to make your body find the way back to where you were BEFORE you stepped into the quicksand.

We Discovered That Quicksand Has Rules:

Quicksand Rule #1: To get out, you have to go back to the safe area.
Quicksand Rule #2: If you don't get out of the quicksand, you will surely die.

This made perfect sense to us. But traveling with a buddy made even more sense to us.

We surmised that generally if you travel with a buddy, that buddy will drag your sorry carcass out of the quicksand with handy rope or a broken tree branch.

We also observed that most of the time a buddy saved the day; or lacking a buddy, even a benevolent wild jungle monkey could save your life in a pinch.

Mostly we saw that those who traveled alone were ON their own in a quicksand crisis.

Quicksand Pits are a lot like being guilty:

- Guilt sucks us down into a pit of despair.
- Guilt confines us.
- Guilt takes all of our options away.

That's why Faithful Friends are a blessing. They come looking for us, and they bring spiritual tools to help get us out of the guilt pit.

Moving on is not always as easy as it sounds, for it sometimes calls for us to live with an unresolved conflict.

Under the best of circumstances, when we sin, we get forgiveness and go on with our lives with the mandate of Doing Better Next Time.

But alas, not all circumstances are like that. Sometimes we have sinned not only against God, but against others. And these "others" may or may not forgive us and be prepared to let the situation pass with ease.

Moving on is a lot like playing a game of cards where there are certain trump cards:

- We play the **first hand** and lose (*due to a sin that we commit*).
- In the **second hand** we ask for mercy and forgiveness from God (*and we receive it*).
- In the **third hand** we confess our sin to the people we have hurt and ask their forgiveness as well (*but it is possible that they may not forgive us*).

- The **fourth hand** can go either way:
  - They may forgive us.
  - They may choose to trump our act of righteousness by withholding forgiveness, (*and if so, we may lose again*).

- But sometimes there is a **fifth hand** in this game; if so, **this is where the highest ranking trump card of the game finally lands in our hands.**
- The name of that card is: **"I Have Done Everything That I Can Do to Make This Right, But Since You Refuse to Accept My Apology, I Don't Care Anymore."**

It's at exactly THAT time, when we suddenly seem to get the highest trump card in the deck (*and thus the upper hand in the situation*), that we may enjoy telling others about how Person X won't forgive despite all the times we have tried to set things right.

The **"I Have Done Everything I Can ... and Don't Care Anymore"** card is a very dangerous card with which to play.

That card is all about false entitlement, resentment, and anger—and therefore it is really best for Christians to stop playing the game before such a card can land in our hands.

Actually it's best to not ever play games with the concept of confession and forgiveness at all; it is not now, nor was it ever a game. The concept of getting the highest trump card in a confession and forgiveness process is yet another example of *The Spider's* Cobwebs that have been intricately spun into the fabric of our society; and it is a win-lose perspective from which Christians would do well to peacefully walk away.

I would also submit that it pays to be very cautious when discussing such confession and forgiveness situations with others, even if the discussion is in the form of a prayer request. Check your heart. Be doubly sure that in the name of asking a friend for prayer support, you are not secretly engaging in a self-serving and/or self-gratifying attempt at blame-casting.

Rather than perpetually keeping the wrong deed or the blame-casting alive by talking about it, it is probably best to simply give the situation and the person involved some space; consider it a RESPECT thing. **And as for seeking those prayer requests from friends, I do need to say that yes sometimes that is exactly the right thing to do.** My point here is to be stone-cold clear about the purity of your motives when seeking others' prayers for a conflict between you and someone else.

Many times it is best to give the situation some time as you personally pray about it before involving anyone else to pray on behalf of the situation. (*And by all means, if you personally are asked to pray for those who are engaged in a difficult confession and forgiveness process, please keep those prayers to yourself so that you will NOT be found staggering headlong into yet another particularly sticky bit of cobweb:* **the pseudo prayer-request gossip circle.)**

Righteousness is both called for and expected.

> **"Therefore confess your sins to each other and pray for each other so that you may be healed. The prayer of a <u>righteous</u> person is powerful and effective."**
>
> JAMES 5:16 (NIV)

If we have honestly confessed and asked forgiveness from a person, we have done our part. The next step is to wait on God to move that person to forgive us.

And we need to be willing to wait. There will certainly be times when a person does not offer forgiveness to us. And when that happens, moving on will be very difficult; but it is an act of faith to be able to do so.

God will touch that person's heart in His Time, not on our time schedule. **(2 Peter 3:8)**

Meanwhile we need to pray for that person to come to peace regarding the situation. And we need to make certain that we are always pleasant and kind and that we are walking worthy of Christ's name as we conduct our daily lives. **(Ephesians 4:1)**

It is important to note that there is a big difference between forgiving and forgetting.

Forgiving is very scriptural and beneficial to the soul. We are told to forgive our brother 70 x 7. **(Matthew 18:21–22)** We are told to forgive as the Lord forgave us. **(Colossians 3:13)** We are told that if we don't forgive others, then God won't forgive us either. **(Matthew 6:14–15)**

(Yet even with all of this scriptural rationale, forgiveness is sometimes a long, painful, and tedious process. It is wise to give yourself and others the time needed to GO through it and GET through it in a spiritually and emotionally healthy way.)

Some people were taught the old adage: Forgive and Forget.

But forgetting is something altogether different from forgiving for this reason: humans do not come equipped with manual ON and OFF switches on their memories.

The memory of an injury, an injustice, or even some degree of ignoble treatment may or may not be something that softens with time. For some people, the pain seems to just fade away, but for others it is ever present and impedes daily function. Christian counselors are terrific allies in facing and working through issues that impede daily lives.

They bring a God-centered approach that can provide comfort, clarity, and compassion in very difficult times; and they tend to be amazingly capable people.

In an effort to be thorough in this biblical discussion, I will point out that there are scriptures that talk about not keeping a record of wrongs, forgetting what is behind, and not letting a bitter root grow up to cause trouble. (**I Corinthians 13:5, Philippians 3:13, Hebrews 12:15**) But to the best of my knowledge, we do not see forgetting as a biblical command.

In addition, I hasten to add that in situations regarding personal safety, even if previous sinful acts have been forgiven, it is wise to be <u>very mindful and very watchful</u> of any person who possesses the potential to harm you or others. (**Matthew 10:16**)

Always remember that sin has consequences and being forgiven does not mean that you will be saved from experiencing the consequences of your sins. This is where the concept of forgetting is given quite a bit of weight. Looking someone in the eye and knowing that they have forgiven you but not forgotten what you did, may very well be a consequence that some people have to live with for a very long time.

There is a consequence for every choice we make (*an action and reaction*), some so small that we don't even register the consequence and others so large that we can't see past the consequence. (*It is important to note that even choices that do NOT involve sin have consequences.*) Some of our choices yield good results. Some yield bad results. Sinning against someone may involve **legal consequences**; TV shows portray those all the time. But what about simple **trust consequences**? These are actually far more common in our daily interactions and can often feel like **high treason** to loved ones.

Thinking that we will be exempted from consequential hardships (*physical, emotional, spiritual, financial, legal and/or **relational***) because we verbally apologize for a wrong word or deed is a very logically flawed perspective.

Adam and Eve sinned when they ate of the forbidden tree in the Garden of Eden, and the consequence of that sin was that they were kicked out of Eden and their lives were forever changed. (**Genesis 3:17-19**) Adam had to toil in the soil for his food and Eve came to know the pain of childbirth.

The Bible shares many stories, positive and negative, about the significance and consequences of our choices (*via thoughts, words, and actions*). Here are just a few:

- Moses was forgiven for "striking the rock" when God told him to "speak to the rock", but as a consequence of the sin of overstepping his instructions in the wilderness, he was not allowed into the Promised Land. (**Numbers 20:12**)
- Uzzah was struck dead because he reached out and took

hold of the Ark of God when the oxen stumbled. Yes, he stabilized the precious Ark, but in so doing, he violated God's rule about not touching it. The consequence was that God struck him down, and he died there beside the Ark of God. **(2 Samuel 6:6–7)**

- Zechariah, father of John the Baptist, was found to be righteous. He and his righteous wife Elizabeth had yearned for many years for a child, yet Elizabeth was barren. One day the angel Gabriel visited Zechariah and told him that he was going to have a son. But when Zechariah doubted the truth of Gabriel's message, he earned a consequence. He was struck mute on that day and was mute for the rest of Elizabeth's pregnancy. Eight days later, at the naming and circumcision gathering, Zechariah was finally able to speak again; he told all assembled that his son's name would be John. **(Luke 1: 5-80)**
- When the widow discreetly gave two small coins in the offering, Jesus knew it was all she had and recognized the sincerity of her sacrifice. **(Luke 21:1–4)**
- Jesus Christ himself endured physical, emotional, and spiritual consequences, not because of sin, but rather as a result of choices that he made. **(Romans 4:25)**

Which brings me to a good point: Jesus fulfilled a lot of prophecy, but he also broke a lot of "rules". Now it is very significant that the rules he broke were man-made not God-made; and Jesus knew the difference. **(Matthew 23:13–39)** He chose to answer to the higher authority, simultaneously drawing strong support from some and cultivating animosity in others.

There may very well be times when you are in the same situation. You may find yourself occasionally caught between just going with the flow of social convention or standing up in opposition against something that you believe to be wrong.

When you stand against something that is wrong, God will be pleased. But you should understand that others may become angry with you. They may accuse you of sinning against them or harming them in some way. Do not be afraid of their anger. Stand up for God, because He is more powerful than the dark forces. But be aware that in standing for up God, you may very well contend with difficult circumstances or even substantially negative consequences.

When Paul and Silas were in Philippi, they were beaten with rods and thrown in jail because they were followers of Christ. Clearly this was a consequence. **(Acts 16: 16–24)** Scripture says that at midnight they were praying and singing hymns when suddenly there was an earthquake. It was so strong that it shook the foundation of the jail, opened all of the jail doors, and shook loose all of the prisoners' chains. **(Acts 16:25)**

The jailer woke up, saw the prison door standing open, assumed that all of the prisoners had escaped, and drew his own sword to use to kill himself. He was prepared to take his own life rather than face the horrible consequence that would be assigned to a Roman jailer who lost all of his prisoners.

Paul prevented his suicide attempt by telling him in a loud voice that all of the prisoners were still in the jail. The jailer called for the lights to be lit, saw the prisoners for himself, and when he came to Paul and Silas he fell down trembling before them.

That night, the jailer and his whole household became Christians. As of result of the words and deeds of Paul and Silas, the jailer took these men who were his prisoners to his very own home where he fed them and washed their wounds. **(Acts 16: 16–34)**

Paul and Silas stood out as men who were different. We should strive to be that kind of different too! Can you imagine the world-changing effect that would be seen if Christians worldwide thought, spoke, and acted with the Spiritual Confidence and Spiritual Concern for others that we see in the story of Paul and Silas at Philippi?

Philippi was a Roman colony, made up of pagans and retired Praetorian Guards. It was a place where well-trained, hard-living, former elite Roman soldiers practiced paganism with all of its sinful rituals; and they flourished there. But Paul and Silas were not afraid. They sang praises at midnight in jail.

Perhaps there is a life lesson here: when the world expects us to be Whining and Wailing in misery, we need to be Singing and Praising God in ecstasy.

The worldwide Christian impact would be utterly amazing!

Chapter 4 Questions for Personal Reflection and Analysis:

A. Is experiencing guilt a good thing or a bad thing? Why?

B. Can you think of a time when experiencing guilt led someone you know to admit their wrongdoing and correct their wrong behavior?

C. What does the New Testament have to say about Guilt and Forgiveness?

D. How did Jesus treat guilty people?

E. How should Christians treat guilty people?

F. What does the phrase "Love the Sinner/Hate the Sin" mean?

G. Can you give an example that would fit that phrase?

H. Does loving a person who is sinning mean that we need to endorse/support their sin?

I. Can you describe any circumstance in which although we might love someone who is sinning, we would need to withdraw from being around him/her?

J. How did the "Woman at the Well" respond to Forgiveness?

K. How did Judas respond to guilt?

L. How did Peter respond to guilt?

M. What is your personal response to guilt? Do you try to cover it up or confess quickly?

N. Have you ever known someone who cannot forgive themselves of something that they have done?

O. Since God is the one who forgives sins, why do you think that some people have a hard time accepting that forgiveness?

P. What is the best approach to help someone who cannot forgive themselves? (Please link these approaches to scripture)

Q. As a friend, have you ever tried to approach someone who is in the spiritual quicksand of quilt? What did you do?

R. How did that person respond?

S. Ultimately what became of that person?

T. How do you think God feels when He forgives a person but that person opts to live in spiritual quicksand because they won't accept His forgiveness as being sufficient to relieve them of their sin?

U. What scriptures did you use as you answered these questions?

Chapter 4 NOTES:

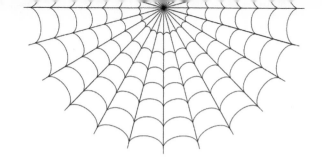

CHAPTER 5

Action Step

LIVE BETTER = PRAY AND STUDY GOD'S WORD

Okay, let's take stock of where you are right now! You understand that Satan acts like a Spider. You understand that he spins wicked-sticky Cobwebs designed to weaken Christian souls. You understand that the Cobwebs have a Cousin called Spiritual Quicksand. And you know that if you Mess Up, you should take the Actions Steps of 'Fess up, Fix it, and Move On. But move on to what? Good question! Let's talk about how to Live Better.

There are a zillion TV gurus out there who have the "secret" to living a better life. Most of those gurus will sell you their secret for the right price. And most of them end up sounding sort of like this...

And wait! There's more!

If you buy *The Big Secret to Living a Better Life* within the next 10 minutes, we will throw in the spiffy watch, the miracle vitamins, the anti-wrinkle cream, the whirling dervish food chopper, and a set of 4 brand new tires. Separate processing and handling charges apply for the tires. Don't Delay Buy Today!!!

But you and I both know that there is no big secret to living a much better life.

There is no secret at all.

It's not even that Hard to live a better life, because there are only three steps in the God-given way to do so:

- **Pray**
- **Study and Follow God's Word**
- **Actively Engage in the Church.**

This chapter is going to address the first two steps in that list.

PRAY:

So it's time to take the plunge here and talk about this concept called prayer.

Bottom Line: God is not Santa Clause!

The creator of the universe is not just sitting around waiting on you to submit your wish list of all the things you want.

However, the creator of the universe DOES want you to talk with Him.

"Then you will call on me and come and pray to me, and I will listen to you."

JEREMIAH 29:12 (NIV°)

For some people, praying is easy; for others it may seem hard. In the course of a lifetime, it is possible to have felt both ways depending on what is going on in your life at the time. God knows that humans experience good times and bad times. Prayer is a special kind of mind and soul-comforting tool that we can use at any time, good or bad; our God designed us to come to him in prayer and share everything that is on our hearts. He never makes us get in line or wait for the person before us to get finished. He never looks at a clock while we talk to Him. Our appointment with Him is never over. And He is never impatient with prayers that don't come to the point immediately because He built us and understands that sometimes it takes people a while to get to the heart of their needs, fears, worries, praises, and thank yous.

The topics you carry to God may be serious ones, but the act of praying is not hard at all.

You can THINK your prayers. You can SAY your prayers. You can WRITE your prayers. The format you choose to use is not nearly as important as your willingness to make contact and share yourself with the Lord.

You can tell God that you don't know where to start, or that you are scared to pray. You can ask Him to help you or someone else. You can tell Him that he did a great job on the sunset today!

I have heard people say that they have trouble with prayer because they don't know what to say; and because of that, they don't try to pray at all.

I have heard people say that they lose their train of thought when they pray; so they just don't pray.

I have heard people say that they feel uncomfortable with the concept of prayer because praying is not something that they grew up doing. Thus, <u>avoiding</u> prayer is preferable to <u>feeling awkward</u> by attempting it.

<u>Here's some help</u>:

- Prayers do not have to be long; there is no required length.
- Prayers do not have to use formal language; God is not offended by short sentences.
- The Bible has "How-To" information about prayer.
- The important thing is to get started by thinking, talking, or writing your prayers to God.

So if:

A. You <u>are someone</u> who feels unsure about how to pray/what to say, OR...

B. You <u>know someone</u> who feels unsure about how to pray/what to say

Here are 10 things that the Bible teaches us about prayer:

1. Jesus himself gave us a sample of HOW to pray to God.

"This, then, is how you should pray: "'Our Father in heaven, hallowed be your name, your kingdom come, your will be done, on earth as it is in heaven. Give us today our daily bread. And forgive us our debts, as we also have forgiven

our debtors. And lead us not into temptation, but deliver us from the evil one. For Yours' is the kingdom and the power and the glory forever. Amen."

Matthew 6:9–13 (NIV°)

2. Jesus also told us WHY to pray.

"Watch and pray so that you will not fall into temptation. The spirit is willing, but the flesh is weak."

Matthew 26:41 (NIV°)

3. King David, of the Old Testament, told us that God LISTENS to us!

"The Lord is near to all who call on him, to all who call on him in truth."

Psalms 145:18 (NIV°)

4. The apostle Paul, of the New Testament, also assured us that when we prayerfully approach God with the perspective of seeking His will, GOD DOES INDEED HEAR US!

"This is the confidence we have in approaching God: that if we ask anything according to his will, he hears us."

1 John 5:14 (NIV°)

5. Paul also took away our anxiety and fear about prayer when he taught us that **OUR SPEAKING ABILITY IS NOT IMPORTANT!** Even if we stutter, stammer, and struggle to find

49

any words at all in our prayers, our God will understand; the Holy Spirit interprets TO and intercedes WITH our God on our behalf. He knows what is really in our hearts.

"In the same way, the Spirit helps us in our weakness. We do not know what we ought to pray for, but the Spirit himself intercedes for us through wordless groans. And he who searches our hearts knows the mind of the Spirit, because the Spirit intercedes for God's people in accordance with the will of God.

ROMANS 8:26–27 (NIV*)

6. Another thing that Paul taught us is that JOY and THANKS-GIVING should be a part of our prayers.

"Rejoice always, pray continually, give thanks in all circumstances; for this is God's will for you in Christ Jesus."

I THESSALONIANS 5:16–18 (NIV*)

7. James, a member of Jesus's earthly family, teaches us that PRAYER WORKS!

"Therefore, confess your sins to each other, and pray for each other so that you may be healed. The prayer of a righteous person is powerful and effective. Elijah was a human being, even as we are. He prayed earnestly that it would not rain, and it did not rain on the land for three and a half years. Again he prayed, and the heavens gave rain, and the earth produced its crops."

JAMES 5:16–18 (NIV*)

8. James also taught us that we must PRAY FOR THE RIGHT REASONS!

"When you ask, you do not receive, because you ask with wrong motives, that you may spend what you get on your pleasures."

JAMES 4:3 (NIV°)

9. Matthew, one of Jesus' Apostles, reminds us that PRAYER IS NOT A SHOW and that we should pray without trying to draw to attention to ourselves.

"And when you pray, do not keep on babbling like pagans, for they think they will be heard because of their many words."

MATTHEW 6:7 (NIV°)

10. Paul adds even more prayer-based clarity for us when in **1 Timothy 2:1** he mentions FOUR CATEGORIES of prayers; and in **1 Timothy 2:2**, he specifies FOR WHOM we should pray. We are to pray for ALL PEOPLE, yes even those with political and/or social positions that exceed our own.

"I urge, then, first of all, that petitions, prayers, intercession and thanksgiving be made for all people—…for kings and all those in authority, <u>that we may live peaceful and quiet lives in all godliness and holiness.</u>"

I TIMOTHY 2:1-2 (NIV°)

(Let's take a little sidestep, and discuss praying for our leaders for bit before we move on to the 4 categories of prayer that Paul addresses in 1 Timothy 2:1–2.)

Regarding praying for our leaders:

I'd like to go on record as saying that regardless of
- political party lines or the lack thereof
- who is president
- who is running for governor
- whether or not I voted for my social club secretary
- whether or not I dislike any elected or appointed official...

Christians ought to act like Christians and not like a pack of barking snarling dogs.

So how should a Christian act *(even a politically active Christian)*?

Here's a quick litmus test for Christians: does anything that you are thinking about, speaking about, or doing resemble a Bowl of Fruit? *(Obviously I am referencing the Fruits of the Spirit found in* **Galatians 5:22–23)**

If not, then perhaps some rethinking, revising, reframing, and re-evaluation of the heart *(and its motivations)* could be needed.

Why? Because if what you are experiencing in your heart *(and its motivations)* is not from God, it very well may be that *The Spider* has convinced you that Righteous Indignation is justification for words and behaviors that do NOT in any way bring glory to God.

As children, many of us were taught that how we acted would reflect on our parents and our family. So it is with Christianity. Our words and deeds matter. And it is important to remember that we, as

Christs Ambassadors (**2 Corinthians 5:18–20**), are called to faithfully represent Him.

(**Sing it with me now:** *"Oh be careful little tongue what you say, oh be care little tongue what you say, for the Father up above is looking down with love, so be careful little tongue what you say."*) [1]

Our God is so incredibly wise to tell us to pray for the people who have earthly power over us. WHY? Because the people who have earthly power over us could decide to use that power to make our lives UNPEACEFUL and UNQUIET. Duh!

So of course it is wise to pray for those who have rank, power and/ or authority.

God's wisdom in this area also shines through in that He does NOT authorize us to talk about them in disrespectful ways. Rather, he instructs us to pray for them.

Now before somebody starts playing patriotic songs in the background and quoting our government documents that guarantee freedom of speech, expression, and assembly, let me assure you that I value my freedoms deeply. (*Those who know me will attest that I exercise my freedom of speech regularly.*)

We Americans tend to exercise our freedoms and liberties in many ways. Freedom and liberty are extremely precious concepts to us. But we have all seen times when someone exercised their freedom of speech with venom in their hearts. Not surprisingly, you may have noticed that venomous speech tends to yield toxic results.

Think about it. When a rattlesnake bites you, the venom that is

---

[1] Lyrics to "Oh Be Careful Little Eyes What You See," accessed June 18, 2018 https://www.hymnal.net/en/hymn/c/157

injected does not enhance you. The snake bites you in order to kill you; to get rid of you. ALL of you.

If we want to bring out the best in our leaders, perhaps we might not want to act like rattlesnakes who have the sole goal of acting out the predator-prey relationship.

Obviously, if I act like a rattlesnake, I should not be surprised when people treat me like a rattlesnake—disdaining me, avoiding me, being fearful of me, and/or even hunting me.

Our American freedoms were not forged to be used as unbridled assault weapons. They were designed to provide every person with the societal tools necessary to keep our way of governmental life balanced; **to keep our county's government representative OF its people rather than reprehensible TO its people.**

But WHO do WE represent? Surely not just our own selves?

No indeed! Christians represent a much greater entity than our own selves.

Take a look at the pattern and conclusion:

- Jesus Christ is the Son of God **(Colossians 1:15)**
- When Jesus Christ was on earth, he represented God. **(John 14:9)**
- Christians are Christ's ambassador's. **(2 Corinthians 5:18–20)**
- Which means that if we are representing Christ as ambassadors and Christ represented God, then our thoughts and words and deeds should be dedicated to accurately representing BOTH Christ AND our Heavenly Father.

Ambassadors work hard at positively representing their homeland.

(You do see where I'm headed with this, don't you?) That's right. This world is NOT our Homeland; Heaven is. REPRESENT!!!

Christians are told that we will be taken to our Father's House **(John 14:4)** and thus it is important that we, as Christians, remember to Represent Our Heavenly Father here on earth—even in those times when we are exercising our American freedoms and liberties.

Christians represent not only Christ, but also Our Father in Heaven, to the world.

This line of thinking does NOT mean that we must just sit and do nothing when we perceive injustice. But rather that in all things, we make certain that we are representing Our Father in doing what needs to be done. All of the words and actions that we undertake should align with what would please Him.

Here's how Jesus handled doing what needed to be done and still represented God:

- Jesus used words *(with no vulgarities)* and actions to stand against authority.
- He based his words and actions on scripture and quoted those scriptures to the people he was addressing.
- He used potent words to itemize the "Seven Woes" associated with the Pharisees, as he itemized exactly what He saw them doing wrong. He called them a brood of vipers and a collection of dead men's bones housed in whitewashed tombs **(Matthew 23:1–39)**
- He knocked over the vendors' tables in the temple because they were **cheating people** in God's House. **(Matthew 21:12)**
- His motives were never self-promoting or self-serving; but

rather, they were exactly what the Father told him to do. **(John 12:49)**

I strongly believe that we should pray for discernment **(Hebrews 5:14)** in order to grasp the difference between the <u>Intent</u> of our words and deeds…and the potential <u>Impact</u> of our words and deeds. As Christians, our freedom to think, speak, and write our opinions is a blessing; but a blessing that is misused can become a curse. Here's a scriptural example of God saying just that!

"If you do not listen, and if you do not resolve to honor my name," says the Lord Almighty, "I will send a curse on you, and I will curse your blessings. Yes, I have already cursed them, because you have not resolved to honor me."

MALACHI 2:2 (NIV®)

How many times have we failed to consider the difference between the intent of our statements/actions and potential impact of our statements/actions? It's hard enough to wisely discern what to say and do in this world when we are actually TRYING to do what is right in God's Eyes. But when *The Spider* has spun us in a web of Anger, Revenge, or perhaps even the most difficult one to control … Righteous Indignation, the results can be atrocious.

There is a significant disconnect when a Christian's words (whether live, recorded, or in printed-word format) are conveyed in a toxic nature from a self-professed Child of God. It is okay to take a stand, but it seems to me that when we stand, we ought to accurately represent the way our God would have us think, speak, and act.

I say that because the Bible clearly tells us that we need to make sure that what comes from us (*our thoughts, words, and deeds*) represents what is within us (*the Holy Spirit*). (**Matthew 7:18, James 3:11**) And Jesus was quite specific about how we are to behave.

> **"But I tell you, love your enemies and pray for those who persecute you, that you may be children of your Father in heaven.** He causes his sun to rise on the evil and the good, and sends rain on the righteous and the unrighteous. If you love those who love you, what reward will you get? Are not even the tax collectors doing that? And if you greet only your own people, what are you doing more than others? Do not even pagans do that? Be perfect, therefore, as your heavenly Father is perfect."
>
> MATTHEW 5:44–48

There may in fact be times when Christians must choose to use hard words and undertake strong actions, but most of the time there is a whole lot of Spiritual Real Estate that lies between Praying <u>for</u> Our Leaders and Actively Crusading <u>against</u> Them. Our God is so wise to tell us to pray for them. For in so doing, we link into EXACTLY what Paul was talking about regarding Petitions, Prayers, Intercessions, and Thanksgiving.

<u>**Matthew Henry's Commentary on 1 Timothy**</u> defines those four words:

Petition (*Supplication* in some translations) - for the averting of evil

Prayers - for the obtaining of good

Intercessions - for others

Thanksgiving - for mercies already received[2]

And yes, we should pray for all of those things. But we do not approach our God with the prayer recipe card and expect that He will bake the cake for which we pray. Prayer isn't like that; it's considerably bigger, deeper, wider, higher, farther and probably many other **"ers"** that you can name to describe the vastness of prayer.

That having been said, some folks enjoy considering the A.C.T.S.[3] approach to prayer to help them keep from being self-centered when they pray. There is no script for this approach. No recipe card. The content of the prayer must be yours alone, but you may find the A.C.T.S. categories helpful. Here's how the A.C.T.S. acronym breaks it down:

Adoration

Praising God. He made heaven and earth, mountain and sea, pine cones and butterflies. He made you; and in so doing He strung the pearls of your DNA. So yeah, it is a wonderful idea to PRAISE HIM for such things.

"And one called out to another; 'Holy, Holy, Holy, is the LORD Almighty; the whole earth is full of His glory.'"

ISAIAH 6:3 (NIV*)

---

[2] Henry, Matthew, and David Winter. 1995. *Matthew Henry's New Testament commentary*. London: Hodder and Stoughton, accessed June 12, 2018 **https://www. biblegateway.com/resources/matthew-henry/2Tim.1.1-2Tim.1.5**

[3] Terhune, Mary Virginia. *Marion Harland*. The Continent. August 8, 1883, accessed June 21, 2018 https://christianity.stackexchange.com/questions/43916/ when-was-the-acronym-acts-first-used-to-refer-to-components-of-prayer

Confession

Yes, *this* DOES include your actions and words. But it also includes your thoughts! It is impossible to convince God of a lie. He knows the truth. And He wants us to learn to Be Honest with HIM, with Others, and with Ourselves.

"The Lord detests lying lips, but he delights in people who are trustworthy."

Proverbs 12:22 (NIV°)

Thanksgiving

Taking the time to mentally itemize each and every blessing that the Lord has provided you is one of the most "depression busting" actions I have ever undertaken. Many have been the times when I thanked God not only for my cup of hot tea, but for the fresh water available to me; and for the money to pay the water bill along with the house with the kitchen that even has running water. You see, when we get to the point of itemizing the HUGE number of blessings we have each day, it's hard to be bummed out about anything else. I challenge you to try to mention EVERY SINGLE THING with which you have been blessed. If you are doing it right, the list will seem almost unending. I have never successfully completed the list; I always find something else for which to thank Him. Not surprisingly, I have found this Thanksgiving Technique to be life-changing!

"Let the message of Christ dwell among you richly as you teach and admonish one another with all wisdom through psalms, hymns, and songs from the Spirit, singing to God with gratitude in your hearts. And whatever you do,

whether in word or deed, do it all in the name of the Lord Jesus, giving thanks to God the Father through him.”

COLOSSIANS 3:16–17 (NIV®)

Supplication

Asking God's protection from evil and harm. I hasten to add that it is important to ask God that you be in His Will in this prayer. God sees a way bigger picture than we do. He knows the future. He knows the past. He knows the present even better than we do. And sometimes, God understands that we must endure some hardships in order to learn and grow in Him. My roots always grow deeper when life's pressures are more intense. I have discovered this: the deeper my spiritual roots are forced to grow, the higher my always faith rises.

“Do not be anxious about anything, but in every situation, by prayer and petition, with thanksgiving, present your requests to God.”

PHILIPPIANS 4:6 (NIV®)

STUDY and FOLLOW GOD'S WORD:

Let's move on to the second portion of this chapter.

There are two ways to protect yourself from *The Spider*:
- Know God's Word
- Follow God's Word

The Bible tells us everything we need to know in order to be able to successfully stand against Satan. Paul, in the book of Ephesians, goes in to great detail to describe how God's Word serves as the uniform for a Christian who is going to have to do battle with an incredible adversary. That Christian is YOU. That Christian is ME. That Christian is Every Christian. We will ALL do battle with Satan. And we know how to win!

The Bible tells us how to protect ourselves.

"Therefore put on the full armor of God, so that when the day of evil comes, you may be able to stand your ground, and after you have done everything, to stand. Stand firm then, with the belt of truth buckled around your waist, with the breastplate of righteousness in place, and with your feet fitted with readiness that comes from the gospel of peace. In addition to all this, take up the shield of faith, with which you can extinguish all the flaming arrows of the evil one. Take the helmet of salvation, and the sword of the Spirit, which is the word of God."

EPHESIANS 6:13–17 (NIV®)

There is a reason why I have shared so many scriptures and quoted so many Bible passages in this book.

It is because the Bible is the **source** for the Action Steps in this book. I am simply giving credit to who said it: The Bible Said It! Plus, I know that these scriptures will help you. They will help others too. That is why I stashed so many of God's Tools in this handy little book. My desire is to help people in their attempts to rid themselves of Spiritual Cobwebs. *(When all of your own spiritual cobwebs are gone, perhaps you'll refer this book to a friend with a similar cobweb issue.)*

Remember: God's Holy Word will supply you with everything you need to know about how to live a better life. You don't need to buy one single thing. It's free but you must read and study it in order to find the tools needed to fight the spiritual battles.

If you follow HIS Instructions, your life will be so richly blessed. To be clear, I am not talking about materialistic blessings, though HE does provide those.

Rather, I am talking about peace of mind. I am talking about personal integrity.

I am talking about faithfulness in marriages, in friendships, and in the workplace.

I am talking about loyalty, honor, and respect. And mostly I am talking about LOVE!

I must also warn you that when we were far from God, *The Spider* had us right where he wanted us. But when we start getting closer to God, Satan will inevitably try to capture us in his sticky spiderwebs and lead us back into that Spiritual Quicksand.

And THAT is why it is so important to not only Know Your Bible, but to also Become Actively Engaged in the Church.

(I do believe that I just saw a lightbulb flickering above your head as you read that last sentence and "connected the dots" about why I mentioned the Quicksand Buddy System in Chapter 4. I love it when I get to see that happen!)

Chapter 5 Questions for Personal Reflection and Analysis:

A. Why do you think television marketing for items that will allegedly help people live better lives is so successful?

B. Can you name some of the persuasion techniques that they use?

C. Do you remember any childhood prayers? Can you still say them?

D. Do you remember who taught you to pray? Did you ever thank that person?

E. Have YOU ever taught anybody to pray?

F. When do you pray?

G. When do you feel drawn to pray? (Daily? Weekly? Only in times of trial?) Why?

H. Is there a specific place where you prefer to pray?

I. What distracts you from prayer?

J. Have you ever had to take steps to stop that distraction?

K. Can you remember a time of JOY-FILLED prayer?

L. Do you have any time that you remember feeling particularly close to God?

M. Do you feel alienated from God?

N. Are you Angry at God? If so, do you know why?

O. Have you tried talking to Him about why you are angry?

P. Do you believe he listens?

Q. Do you believe he cares?

R. Are there people you pray for?

S. Are there people who pray for you?

T. Do you pray for your bosses, colleagues, peers?

U.   Do you pray for your country, the president, governor, mayor, etc.?

V.   Do you pray for our schools and our children?

W.   Have you ever thought that God ANSWERED your prayer with YES?

X.   Have you ever thought that God ANSWERED your prayer with NO?

Y.   Have you ever thought that God ANSWERED your prayer with NOT YET?

Z.   How many blessings are on your list of things for which to be thankful?

AA. What scriptures did you use as you answered these questions?

Chapter 5 NOTES:

CHAPTER 6

Action Step

BE ACTIVELY ENGAGED
IN THE CHURCH

*This is the last and culminating chapter of this book. Now I do
understand that for most authors, the last chapter is where we
see the book's final resolution of all tension. It is where the results
of all of our "reader angst" is made worthwhile. But I am NOT
most authors. This final chapter is not THE Final Chapter. (But
this is where things really get cookin'.) Being Actively Engaged
in the Church is not a box we check. It is not a pin in a map
marking a destination that we have reached. To me, it's a whole
lot more like being in an airport.*

L et's talk about airports for bit. When strangers enter airports, they
enter a center of activity. There is movement. There is action. There
is noise. People are laughing, people are crying, and little kids are

running around. There are lots of smiles, hugs, and sometimes there are obvious disagreements.

At airports you will see people walking, at various speeds, toward a place where they will sit for a period of time while they wait to enter their plane. The goal as they wait is to just get comfortable. Meanwhile, you will see some folks who read and others who are listening to music. If you look around you'll also notice that some people close their eyes and rest, while others seem to delight in "people watching." There are usually a whole lot of people playing games on cell phones and you'll find a lot of people chatting away.

Eventually this collection of humans will walk through a doorway and enter a plane. Once everybody is seated, that plane will start moving faster and faster down the runway. And then you know exactly what will happen. If that plane is moving fast enough, even while carrying the weight of the fuel, the people, and all of their baggage, it will become airborne. Then everybody on that plane will ascend heavenward.

All of the things that used to look so big will get smaller and smaller until they disappear completely.

We are all travelers on an incredible journey. Along the way, we get to see amazing things. We get to experience mouthwatering foods and see breathtaking vistas. But there is nothing that we can experience here on earth that will escape being totally eclipsed by the glory of our God.

And because of that, I want to be on that plane that goes heavenward. And because of that, I am willing to embrace, support, and uplift the whole gamut of human frailty seen in my local congregation. Moreover, I pray that aforementioned gamut of human frailty, otherwise known as my church family, is willing to embrace, support, and uplift me too. Without them I would be ill-equipped to meet the challenges that this world puts me through. We meet each Sunday for the purpose of taking Communion and being in communion with our Lord Jesus Christ; and in communion with each other. We are actively in each other's lives. Like family.

In Chapter 3 we discussed **Fix It! (Even If You Can't God Can!).** In Chapter 4 we discussed Spiritual Quicksand and the wisdom of traveling with a buddy to help in times of trouble. **Amazingly, both of these topics were addressed 2000 years ago!**

When Jesus Christ died for our sins, rose from the dead, and then established the Church, that was God's Biggest FIX ever! God FIXED the sin that separated us in the Garden of Eden, He FIXED the sin that separated us from Him eternally, and He sacrificed His only son Jesus in order to do it. Don't forget that Jesus went along with the plan when he surrendered his own will.

> **"Going a little farther, he fell with his face to the ground and prayed, 'My Father, if it is possible, may this cup be taken from Me. Yet not as I will, but as you will.'"**
> **MATTHEW 26:39 (NIV°)**

God knew that we are all going to struggle with sin and so He built a plan that solved the issue of sin once and for all. And once having conquered death, Jesus presented the Church to the world. So here we sit waiting for our plane. (*Churches really are a lot like airports.*) The people you wait with at the airport are traveling with you. They are the ones who will be with you for your journey. They are your buddies.

So make the most of it while you live your life. Don't sit around being lonely. Connect with others. Become actively engaged in the lives of other members of the Church.

Merely attending church will leave you feeling unfulfilled and undervalued. We need to Actively Participate and become vested in doing the Lord's Work while we wait. Get to know others and let them get to know you as well.

The Cobwebs and Quicksand are always nearby, so get busy and build yourself a really strong Buddy System. You will be helping others and they will be helping you. Social interaction and bonding takes time. It requires effort. So go shake hands with someone you don't know at church and talk to people. If you see someone new at church, go introduce yourself to them and shake their hand. Maybe you can invite them to go to lunch after church. You can call, text, or email them. Just make the effort to connect. Make the effort to engage with the activities already planned at church. Invite people. Isn't it amazing that somehow when you **TAKE** the time to connect with others, they somehow **MAKE** the time to connect with you too?

Good System, huh! Yeah, our God is SMART like that.

There is a reason why **Hebrews 10:23–25 (NIV®)** says,

"Let us hold unswervingly to the hope we profess, for he who promised is faithful. And let us consider how we may spur one another on toward love and good deeds, <u>not giving up meeting together, as some are in the habit of doing</u>, but encouraging one another—and all the more as you see the Day approaching."

The reason we go to church is because it brings us closer to God and closer to others. It brings us deep and abiding friends, but that does not happen by simply walking in the door, going through the motions, singing the songs, taking Communion, listening to the preacher, and the going home to a life filled with Cobwebs and Quicksand. We need each other. We need to share our strengths and our weaknesses. It's what family does.

– We all need buddies we can rely on.

– We all need people to share our joys and our struggles.

– God made us, and He knows our needs.

– Jesus gave us the Church, where those needs are lovingly met.

We are all waiting to ride that plane and we all have the opportunity to enjoy the waiting time in the presence of the Family of God. So I urge you, if you have not already done so, get yourself plugged into an active church as soon as possible.

"The Spirit himself testifies with our spirit that we are God's children. Now if we are children, then we are heirs-heirs of God and co-heirs with Christ, if indeed we share in his sufferings in order that we may also share in his glory."

Roman 8:16–17 (NIV®)

Christians are the Family of God;
Go to Church
and
Find More of Your Family.

(It'll zap *The Spider* AND help you with that icky Cobweb trouble!☺)

Chapter 6 Questions for Personal Reflection and Analysis:

A. Do want to have a church home?

B. How will you go about selecting a congregation?

C. Do you feel close to the pulpit minister of your congregation?

D. Do you feel close to any of the members of your congregation?

E. Do you think you would benefit from visiting with people in their homes?

F. If you would like to grow deeper in your spiritual journey, do you know who to contact in your congregation?

G. Do you have a Bible Reading Schedule?

H. Do you attend any midweek Bible Studies?

I. Have you invited any of your friends outside the Church to come with you?

J. If not, why not?

K. What would help you be able to invite them?

L. Are you Familiar with Bible Apps to enhance your personal Bible Study?

M. If you have a cell phone or computer, have you ever used Bible Gateway?

Chapter 6 NOTES:

SCRIPTURES CITED

IN THIS BOOK:

Old Testament Verses	New Testament Verses
Genesis 3:17–19	Matthew 5:23–24
Numbers 20:12	Matthew 5:44–48
1 Samuel 13:14	Matthew 6:7
2 Samuel 6:6–7	Matthew 6:9–13
2 Samuel 12:10–14	Matthew 6:14–15
Isaiah 6:3	Matthew 7:18
Jeremiah 29:12	Matthew 10:16
Psalms 145:18	Matthew 18:7–9
Proverbs 15:1	Matthew 18:21–22
Proverbs 12:22	Matthew 18:21–35
Malachi 2:2	Matthew 21:12
	Matthew 23:1–39
	Matthew 23:13–39
	Matthew 26:41
	Mark 11:25
	Luke 1:5–80
	Luke 8:17
	Luke 21:1–4
	John 12:49
	John 12:49
	John 14:4
	John 14:9
	Acts 16:25
	Romans 3:23
	Romans 4:25

	Romans 6:1–2
	Romans 8:16–18
	Romans 8:26–27
	Romans 12:18
	1 Corinthians 10:14
	1 Corinthians 13:5
	2 Corinthians 5:18–20
	Galatians 3:13–15
	Galatians 5:22–23
	Ephesians 4:1
	Ephesians 4:26
	Ephesians 5:8
	Ephesians 6:13–17
	Philippians 3:13
	Philippians 4:6
	Philippians 4:8–11
	Colossians 1:9–10
	Colossians 1:15
	Colossians 3:2
	Colossians 3:16–17
	I Thessalonians 5:16–18
	I Timothy 2:1–2
	Hebrews 4:12
	Hebrews 5:14
	Hebrews 10:24–25
	Hebrews 12:15
	James 3:11
	James 3:12
	James 4:3
	James 5:16
	James 5:16–18
	2 Peter 3:8
	I John 1:7
	I John 1:9
	I John 5:14

Bibliography

1. Henry, Matthew, and David Winter. 1995. *Matthew Henry's New Testament commentary*. London: Hodder and Stoughton, accessed June 12, 2018 **https://www.biblegateway.com/resources/matthew-henry/2Tim.1.1-2Tim.1.5**

2. *Holy Bible*. New International Version, Zondervan Press, 2011. Grand Rapids, MI. 49546, USA

3. Lyrics to "Oh Be Careful Little Eyes What You See," accessed June 18, 2018 **https://www.hymnal.net/en/hymn/c/157**

4. Terhune, Mary Virginia. *Marion Harland*. The Continent. August 8, 1883

CPSIA information can be obtained
at www.ICGtesting.com
Printed in the USA
LVHW112156220319
611588LV00001B/1/P

9 781595 559098